MARKS &
SPENCER

finger food

simple and delicious easy-to-make recipes

Bernice Hurst

Marks and Spencer p.l.c.
Baker Street,
London, WIU 8EP
www.marksandspencer.com.

ISBN: 1-84273-275-7

Printed in Spain

Produced by The Bridgewater Book Company Ltd.

Photographer Ian Parsons
Home Economist Sara Hesketh

COVER
Photographer Ian Parsons
Home Economist Sara Hesketh

NOTES FOR THE READER

- This book uses both metric and imperial measurements. Follow the same units of measurement throughout; do not mix metric and imperial.
- All spoon measurements are level: teaspoons are assumed to be 5 ml, and tablespoons are assumed to be 15 ml.
- Unless otherwise stated, milk is assumed to be full fat, eggs and individual vegetables such as potatoes are medium, and pepper is freshly ground black pepper.
- Recipes using raw or very lightly cooked eggs should be avoided by infants, the elderly, pregnant women, convalescents, and anyone suffering from an illness.
- Optional ingredients, variations or serving suggestions have not been included in the calculations. The times given are an approximate guide only. Preparation times differ according to the techniques used by different people and the cooking times vary as a result of the type of oven used.

contents

introduction

Nibbling snacks, starters or canapés affords a particular satisfaction that eating formal knife-and-fork food can't beat. As in countries where large dishes are shared and dipped into with fingers or chunks of bread, most of us instinctively revert to eating with our hands whenever the opportunity arises.

Modern barbecues generally feature food that can be picked up and eaten instantly – burgers, spareribs, chicken pieces, anything on a stick.

The short time allocated for lunch when at work or school, or the pleasure of a picnic on a warm summer's day, lend themselves to pies, tarts and pastries, not to mention encouraging creativity in sandwich-making. Filling a crusty roll or baguette, or thick slices of fresh bread, with whatever combinations come to hand, makes a delicious and frequently nutritious way of pleasurably satisfying the appetite.

Our finger food recipes are suitable for all sorts of occasions. They are good enough to serve to guests and equally suitable for lunch boxes or casual family lunches and suppers. Many are fine on their own, but a combination, served all at once in the style of a Middle Eastern mezze, makes for even more fun.

guide to recipe key		
	easy	Recipes are graded as follows: 1 pea = easy; 2 peas = very easy; 3 peas = extremely easy.
	serves 4	Recipes generally serve four people. Simply halve the ingredients to serve two, taking care not to mix imperial and metric measurements.
	15 minutes	Preparation time. Where chilling food is involved, the necessary time has been added on separately: eg, 15 minutes + 30 minutes to chill.
	15 minutes	Cooking time.

vegetable cream dip
page 16

stuffed tomatoes
page 32

goat's cheese & chive croûtons
page 50

chorizo & olive frittata
page 66

dips & spreads

Dips and spreads are simple, versatile fast food. Raw vegetables and crisps taste great with Easy Onion Dip, Hummus, Taramasalata or Guacamole. And Smoked Fish Pâté or Grandma's Chopped Herring spread lavishly on toast or crackers makes a brilliant lunch or light supper – or even the first course of a special dinner. You can also pack little tubs into a picnic or lunch box for a delicious portable banquet – the possibilities are endless.

hummus

		ingredients
easy		115 g/4 oz dried chickpeas GARNISH
		cold water, to cover 1 tbsp olive oil
serves 4		3–6 tbsp lemon juice 1 tsp cayenne pepper or paprika
		3–6 tbsp water 1 tbsp chopped fresh parsley
		2–3 garlic cloves, peeled and crushed or coriander
15 minutes + 1 hour to chill		140 g/5 oz tahini
		salt
1 hour		

Soak the chickpeas overnight in enough cold water to cover them and allow room for expansion. Drain the chickpeas and boil in fresh water until tender – about 1 hour. Drain.

To make the hummus, put the chickpeas into a food processor and blend with enough lemon juice and water to make a thick, smooth purée.

Add the garlic cloves. Mix well. Add the tahini and salt to taste. Add more lemon juice or water if necessary to get the flavour and consistency that you want.

Spoon into a serving dish, drizzle over the olive oil and sprinkle with either cayenne or paprika. Garnish with the chopped parsley or coriander.

Cover with clingfilm and chill for at least 1 hour before serving.

taramasalata

		ingredients	
very easy		55 g/2 oz white bread	pinch of cayenne pepper
		milk, to soak	3–6 tbsp lemon juice
serves 4		75 g/2¾ oz smoked cod's roe	2–4 tbsp oil
		1 garlic clove, crushed	
10 minutes			
—			

Remove the crusts from the bread and soak in the milk for about 5 minutes, or until soft. Squeeze dry, reserving the liquid.

Combine the cod's roe, bread, garlic and cayenne in a food processor and blend until smooth. Slowly add the lemon juice and oil, tasting frequently. Add the milk that was used to soak the bread if the consistency is not quite smooth enough.

Transfer the taramasalata to a serving dish. If not using immediately, cover with clingfilm and refrigerate until 30 minutes before you need it.

sesame aubergine dip

		ingredients	
very easy			
serves 4	1 medium aubergine 4–6 tbsp olive oil juice of 1–2 lemons		4–6 tbsp tahini 1–2 garlic cloves, crushed 1 tsp sesame seeds, to garnish
10 minutes			
15 minutes			

Place the aubergine on a preheated griddle or under the grill and cook, turning frequently, until the skin is black and blistered. The aubergine itself will be very soft.

Transfer to a chopping board and leave to cool slightly. Cut it in half and scoop out the inside into a mixing bowl. Mash with a fork to make a coarse paste.

Gradually add the olive oil, lemon juice, tahini and garlic. Mix well, tasting until you achieve the flavour and texture you like.

Transfer the mixture to an attractive bowl and serve at room temperature. If not using immediately, cover with clingfilm and refrigerate until 30 minutes before you need it.

Just before serving, toss the sesame seeds in a very hot, dry frying pan for a few seconds to toast them. Sprinkle over the aubergine spread to garnish.

guacamole

		ingredients	
	very easy	2 ripe avocados	2 tbsp fresh coriander, chopped finely
		1 tomato	1 tbsp fresh red or green chilli,
	serves 4	juice of 1 lime	deseeded and chopped finely
		1 tbsp sweet onion, chopped finely	(optional)
	10 minutes		
	—		

Cut the avocados in half, discard the stones and scoop the pulp into a large bowl. Mash to make a coarse paste.

Cut the tomato in half and remove all the seeds. Dice the flesh and add to the avocados.

Stir in the lime juice to loosen the mixture slightly, then stir in the onion, coriander and chilli. Spoon into an attractive bowl and serve immediately.

vegetable cream dip

		ingredients	
	very easy	225 g/8 oz cream cheese	1 tbsp fresh parsley, chopped finely
		125 ml/4 fl oz natural yogurt	1 tbsp fresh thyme, chopped finely
	serves 4	or soured cream	2 spring onions, chopped finely
	5 minutes		
	—		

Beat the cream cheese in a large mixing bowl until it is soft and smooth.

Add the yogurt (or soured cream, if using), herbs and one spring onion. Mix well.

Cover with clingfilm and refrigerate for at least 30 minutes. Stir thoroughly before transferring to a serving dish.

Sprinkle the remaining spring onion over the top of the dip to garnish before serving.

smoked fish pâté

		ingredients
extremely easy		350 g/12 oz smoked mackerel, skinned and boned 175 g/6 oz butter, melted 125 ml/4 fl oz double cream	3 tbsp lemon juice salt and pepper pinch of cayenne pepper
serves 4			
10 minutes + at least 1 hour to chill			
—			

Put the fish into a food processor and blend with half of the melted butter to a smooth paste.

Transfer the mixture into a bowl and gradually add the remaining butter, along with the cream and lemon juice, and season to taste.

Spoon into a serving dish and sprinkle with cayenne pepper.

Cover with clingfilm and chill for at least 1 hour before serving.

easy onion dip

		ingredients
	extremely easy	225 ml/8 fl oz soured cream
	serves 4	3 tbsp dried onion flakes
		2 beef stock cubes, crumbled
	5 minutes + at least 30 minutes to chill	
	—	

Combine the ingredients in a small bowl and mix very well.

Cover with clingfilm and refrigerate for at least 30 minutes.

Stir thoroughly before transferring to a serving dish.

grandma's chopped herring

		ingredients
very easy		4 rollmops, with onions
serves 4		2 hardboiled eggs
		1 cooking apple
10 minutes		1 tbsp matzoh meal
—		or fine breadcrumbs

Skin the rollmops and chop with the onions, eggs and apple.

Mix in the matzoh meal and turn into a serving dish. If not using immediately, cover with clingfilm and refrigerate until 10 minutes before you need it.

new york
chopped liver

		ingredients
easy		3 tbsp chicken fat, diced
		1 onion, chopped finely
serves 4		225 g/8 oz chicken livers
		2 hardboiled eggs
		salt and pepper
10 minutes		
10 minutes		

Place the chicken fat and 1 tablespoon of the onion in a frying pan. Cook over a medium heat until the fat has melted and the remaining bits are very brown and crisp. Drain the crispy bits and set aside.

Sauté the chicken livers and the rest of the onion, chopped coarsely, in the hot chicken fat.

Drain the liver carefully, reserving the fat. Cool for a few minutes, then chop finely or mince, along with the onion and eggs. If you use a food processor, do not let the mixture get too smooth.

Spoon the liver mixture into a bowl and season to taste. Stir in the reserved crisp onions and just enough of the liquid chicken fat to bind. Transfer to a serving dish, cover with clingfilm and refrigerate until 10 minutes before serving.

cheese ball assortment

		ingredients	
very easy		**BLUE CHEESE BALLS**	3 tbsp dry sherry or Martini
		115 g/4 oz blue cheese, crumbled	few drops of Worcestershire sauce
serves 4		125 ml/4 fl oz soured cream	2 tbsp spring onions or chives,
		2 tbsp spring onions or chives,	chopped finely
		chopped finely	1 tbsp finely chopped celery
20 minutes		1 tbsp finely chopped celery	
+ 1 hour			**FETA CHEESE BALLS**
to chill		**CREAM CHEESE BALLS**	115 g/4 oz Feta cheese, crumbled
		115 g/4 oz farmhouse cheese	115 g/4 oz butter, softened
—		(eg Cheddar, Lancashire), grated	½ tsp paprika
		85 g/3 oz cream cheese	2 tbsp finely chopped fresh herbs

To make the blue cheese balls, mash the cheese and mix with the soured cream to make a smooth paste. Add the spring onions and celery. With wet hands, take small spoonfuls of the mixture and form into balls. Arrange on a plate, cover with clingfilm and chill.

To make the cream cheese balls, mash the farmhouse cheese with the cream cheese to make a smooth paste. Season with sherry or Martini and with Worcestershire sauce. Fold in the spring onions and celery. Shape and chill as above.

To make the feta cheese balls, mash the cheese with the butter to make a smooth paste. Season with paprika and herbs, shape and chill as above.

Any of the balls can be rolled in chopped nuts, shredded ham, minced green or red pepper, celery or fresh herbs. A platter of assorted coatings makes a delicious and attractive hors d'œuvre.

stuffed vegetables

Stuffed vegetables can be eaten hot or cold, raw or cooked, filled with any combination of ingredients that you have available or feel inspired by. Try serving Stuffed Mushrooms or Celery with Olive Cheese Filling as elegant hors d'œuvre or canapés for a drinks or dinner party. And Stuffed Tomatoes and Stuffed Peppers make excellent picnic or lunch box snacks. They can even be used as a main course for a summer lunch or supper. Sauces for dipping can be added to provide that extra little something – turning a quick dish into a firm favourite.

stuffed mushrooms

		ingredients	
	very easy	450 g/1 lb button mushrooms	25 g/1 oz fresh white breadcrumbs
		2 tbsp minced onion	1 tsp chopped fresh parsley
	serves 4	3 garlic cloves	1 tbsp grated Parmesan cheese
		175 g/6 oz butter	
	15 minutes		
	20 minutes		

Preheat the oven to 180°C/350°F/Gas Mark 4.

Remove the mushroom stems and chop finely. Mix with the onion and 2 finely chopped cloves of garlic.

Melt half of the butter over a medium heat in a heavy frying pan. Cook the mushroom stems, onion and garlic for 3 minutes, or until softened. In a small bowl, combine the breadcrumbs, parsley and cheese. Stir into the hot onion mixture. Place a small spoonful in each mushroom cap.

Melt the remaining butter in a small pan. Mince the remaining clove of garlic and toss in the butter for 2 minutes. Pour half into a shallow ovenproof dish.

Arrange the stuffed mushroom caps in the dish, pour over the remaining butter and place the dish in the oven. Bake for 20 minutes. Serve hot.

stuffed tomatoes

		ingredients	
easy		2 tbsp butter, melted	115 g/4 oz rice
serves 4		25 g/1 oz pine kernels	225 ml/8 fl oz chicken stock
		8 water chestnuts, sliced	4 medium or 8 small tomatoes
10 minutes			
20 minutes			

Melt the butter in a medium-sized pan over a medium heat. Toss in the pine kernels, water chestnuts and rice. Stir to coat. Add the stock, cover and cook gently for about 20 minutes, or until all the liquid is absorbed and the rice is soft. Leave to cool.

Slice the top off the tomatoes and scoop out the seeds. Fill with the cooked rice mixture and serve at room temperature.

stuffed peppers

		ingredients
	very easy	4 red, yellow or green peppers
	serves 4	115 g/4 oz cream cheese ½ tsp lemon juice 55 g/2 oz smoked salmon salt and pepper
	15 minutes + 3–4 hours to chill	
	—	

Cut a thick slice off the top of the peppers and carefully remove all the seeds.

Beat the cream cheese with the lemon juice until light and smooth. Add the diced or minced salmon and blend thoroughly. Season to taste with salt and pepper.

Fill the peppers with cheese, packing it in gently. Cover with clingfilm and chill for 3–4 hours.

To serve the peppers, unwrap them and cut into thin slices horizontally. Arrange overlapping slices on an attractive platter.

celery with olive
cheese filling

		ingredients	
	very easy	12 sticks of celery	2 spring onions, chopped finely
		225 g/8 oz cream cheese	1 tbsp finely chopped fresh parsley
	serves 4	55 g/2 oz black or green olives, stoned and chopped finely	2 tsp Tabasco or hot pepper sauce, optional
		55 g/2 oz pimento, chopped finely	
	10 minutes		
	—		

Top and tail the celery sticks, removing all the leaves and any rough strings.

Beat the cream cheese in a mixing bowl until soft and smooth. Add all the other ingredients and mix well.

Spoon or pipe the cream cheese into the celery stalks. Cut the sticks into 5 cm/2 inch pieces and arrange on an attractive serving dish.

pastries
& toasties

There are as many different pastries and breads to choose from – plain or flavoured, short or flaky, crusty or soft – as ways in which to use them. The recipes that follow should set your creative juices flowing – Miniature Onion Pizzas, Feta & Tomato Triangles, Olive & Tomato Bruschetta or Broccoli Cashew Tarts. Experiment with these and invent your own alternatives for delicious treats at any time of the day.

cheese straws

		ingredients
	very easy	flour, to roll out
	serves 4	225 g/8 oz puff pastry
		2 tsp mustard, optional
	5 minutes	115 g/4 oz grated cheese
		cayenne pepper, optional
	10 minutes	

Preheat the oven to 200°C/400°F/Gas Mark 6.

Sprinkle your work surface with flour, then roll out the pastry to make a large rectangle.

Spread the mustard, cheese and cayenne (if using) over the pastry, then cut it into thin strips about 10 cm/4 inches long.

Carefully arrange the straws on a greased baking tray, transfer to the oven and bake for 5–10 minutes, or until crisp and golden.

Remove from the oven, leave to cool and then serve in baskets or piled high on plates.

speciality bread crisps

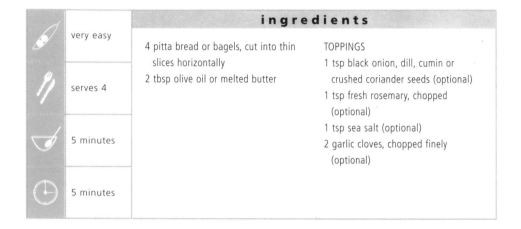

very easy	
serves 4	
5 minutes	
5 minutes	

ingredients

4 pitta bread or bagels, cut into thin
slices horizontally
2 tbsp olive oil or melted butter

TOPPINGS
1 tsp black onion, dill, cumin or
crushed coriander seeds (optional)
1 tsp fresh rosemary, chopped
(optional)
1 tsp sea salt (optional)
2 garlic cloves, chopped finely
(optional)

Preheat the oven to 200°C/400°F/Gas Mark 6.

Brush the pitta bread with oil or butter and sprinkle with
whichever toppings you have decided to use.

Arrange the bread on a baking tray and heat in the oven for
5 minutes, or until crispy and golden. Remove from the oven,
cut into fingers or triangles and serve immediately with a
selection of Dips & Spreads (see pages 6–27).

miniature onion pizzas

<table>
<tr><td>very easy</td><td colspan="2">ingredients</td></tr>
<tr><td rowspan="2">serves 4</td><td>115 g/4 oz strong white bread flour,
  plus flour for kneading
½ tsp easy blend dried yeast
½ tsp salt
1 tbsp olive oil
125–225 ml/4–8 fl oz warm water</td><td>TOPPING
4 tbsp olive oil
1 large onion, sliced thinly
1 tsp brown sugar
1 tsp balsamic vinegar
55 g/2 oz feta, mozzarella or
  Gorgonzola cheese, grated or sliced</td></tr>
<tr></tr>
</table>

1¼ hours

10 minutes

Mix the flour, yeast and salt in a bowl. Drizzle over half of the oil. Make a well in the flour and pour in the water. Mix to a firm ball of dough. Turn it out onto a floured work surface and knead until it is no longer sticky. Add more flour if necessary. Grease the bowl with the remaining oil. Return the dough to the bowl, turn once to coat, cover with a clean tea towel and leave to rise for 1 hour.

Heat the oil for the topping in a pan over a medium heat. Add the onion and cook for 10 minutes. Sprinkle with sugar and cook for 5 minutes more, stirring occasionally. Add the vinegar and cook for 5 more minutes. Remove from the heat and leave to cool.

Preheat the oven to 220°C/425°F/Gas Mark 7. When the dough has doubled, punch it down to release excess air, knead until smooth, then divide in quarters and roll out into thin circles. Place the dough on a baking sheet, spread with onions and top with cheese. Bake for 10 minutes. Remove from the oven and serve.

spinach, feta
& tomato triangles

		ingredients	
very easy			
serves 4	2 tbsp olive oil	2 sheets filo pastry	
	2 tbsp finely chopped shallot	115 g/4 oz feta cheese, crumbled	
	115 g/4 oz fresh spinach, washed	6 sun-dried tomatoes, chopped finely	
20 minutes	and shredded	115 g/4 oz butter, melted	
	salt and pepper		
10 minutes			

Preheat the oven to 200°C/400°F/Gas Mark 6. Heat the oil in a pan over a medium heat and cook the shallot for 2–3 minutes. Add the spinach, increase the heat to high and cook, stirring constantly, for 2–3 minutes. Remove from the heat and drain. Chop coarsely, season to taste and leave to cool.

Cut each sheet of pastry into 6 strips. Place a spoonful of spinach at the bottom of each strip. Scatter cheese and tomatoes on top. Fold the bottom right-hand corner of each strip up to meet the opposite side to form a triangle. Fold the triangle towards the top of the strip and repeat until you reach the top of the strip.

Brush the edges of each triangle with melted butter, then transfer to a greased baking tray. Brush the top of the parcel with more butter. Place the baking tray in the oven and bake for 10 minutes, or until the pastry is golden and crispy. Remove from the oven and serve at once.

olive & tomato
bruschetta

		ingredients	
	very easy	125 ml/4 fl oz extra virgin olive oil	6 leaves fresh basil, torn
	serves 4	1 small oval-shaped loaf of white bread (ciabatta or bloomer), cut into 1 cm/½ inch slices	salt and pepper
			8 black olives, pitted and chopped
	10 minutes	4 tomatoes, deseeded and diced	1 large garlic clove, peeled and halved
	5 minutes		

Pour half of the oil into a shallow dish and place the bread in it. Leave for 1–2 minutes, then turn and leave for an additional 2 minutes. The bread should be thoroughly saturated in oil.

Meanwhile, put the tomatoes in a mixing bowl. Sprinkle the basil leaves over the tomatoes. Season to taste with salt and pepper. Add the olives. Pour over the remaining olive oil and leave to marinate while you toast the bruschetta.

Preheat the grill to medium. Place the bread on the grill rack and cook until golden and crispy – about 2 minutes on each side.

Remove the bread from the grill and arrange on a serving dish.

Rub the cut edge of the garlic halves over the surface of the bruschetta, then top each slice with a spoonful of the tomato mixture. Serve as soon as possible.

goat's cheese
& chive croûtons

		ingredients
	very easy	125 ml/4 fl oz extra virgin olive oil
		8 x 1 cm/½ inch thick slices of
	serves 4	baguette or ciabatta
		115 g/4 oz goat's cheese
		black pepper
	5 minutes	1 tbsp fresh chives, snipped finely
	10 minutes	

Pour the oil into a shallow dish and place the bread in it. Leave for 1–2 minutes, then turn and leave for an additional 2 minutes. The bread should be thoroughly saturated in oil.

Meanwhile, if the cheese has come in a log, cut into 8 slices. If it has come in rounds, crumble coarsely.

Preheat the oven to 180°C/350°F/Gas Mark 4. Place the bread on a baking tray in the oven for 5 minutes. Remove the tray from the oven, turn the bread over and top each slice with cheese. Sprinkle generously with black pepper.

Return the tray to the oven for a further 5 minutes to heat the cheese thoroughly. Remove from the oven, arrange the croûtons on plates and sprinkle with chives. Serve immediately.

broccoli cashew tart

		ingredients	
	very easy	225 g/8 oz shortcrust or cheese pastry	50 ml/2 fl oz milk
	serves 6–8	450 g/1 lb broccoli, cut into florets	85 g/3 oz cheese (eg, Cheddar, Emmenthal, Parmesan, Gruyère), grated roughly
		55 g/2 oz unsalted cashew nuts, chopped	salt and pepper
	45 minutes	55 g/2 oz butter	1 egg
		55 g/2 oz plain flour	pinch of cayenne pepper
	25 minutes		

Preheat the oven to 200°C/400°F/Gas Mark 6. Roll out the pastry on a lightly floured surface and line a 23 cm/9 inch shallow pie dish and bake blind. Remove from the oven and leave to cool.

Steam the broccoli for 5 minutes. Remove and chop coarsely. Spread over the pastry case. Season, then sprinkle with nuts.

Melt the butter in a pan over a medium heat. Stir in the flour. Gradually add the milk, stirring, until the sauce has thickened. Season to taste. Add the grated cheese and cook until melted.

Separate the egg. Stir 2 tablespoons of cheese sauce into the yolk, then add to the sauce and mix. Remove from the heat. Whisk the egg white until stiff. Fold into the cheese sauce. Pour the sauce over the broccoli and spread gently. Sprinkle with cayenne pepper. Place the dish on a baking tray and bake for 20 minutes. Remove from the oven and leave for 5 minutes to rest before cutting.

spinach & potato puff

very easy	
serves 4	
25 minutes	
30 minutes	

ingredients

350 g/12 oz small new potatoes, cooked, peeled and cut into thick slices
350 g/12 oz puff pastry
flour, to roll out
450 g/1 lb fresh spinach or Swiss chard, washed thoroughly

½ tsp finely grated nutmeg
225 g/8 oz mozzarella cheese, sliced or grated
salt and pepper
1 egg
1 tbsp water

Prepare the potatoes and set aside. Cut the pastry into two pieces, one twice as large as the other. Roll the pastry out on a floured surface and trim into 2 rectangles. Keep the trimmings and let the pastry rest for 10 minutes.

Cook the spinach in a pan over a medium heat for 3–4 minutes. Drain, chop and season to taste with salt, pepper and nutmeg.

Arrange a layer of potatoes on the larger rectangle, leaving a margin of pastry on all sides. Season to taste. Spread the spinach over the potatoes. Top with cheese and a final layer of potatoes.

Beat the egg and stir in the water. Fold the margins of the pastry to the centre. Brush with egg. Put the smaller rectangle on top and seal. Transfer to a greased baking tray. Brush with egg. Roll out the trimmings and cut into shapes. Place on top of the pastry parcel and brush with egg. Bake for 30 minutes. Remove from the oven. Leave to rest for 5 minutes before slicing and serving.

basil courgette
toasties

easy	
serves 4	
10 minutes	
45 minutes	

ingredients

4 slices of white bread
55 g/2 oz butter, melted
4 eggs
450 ml/16 fl oz milk
1 small onion, chopped finely
1 courgette, grated

115 g/4 oz grated cheese
115 g/4 oz fresh breadcrumbs
1 tbsp finely chopped fresh basil
salt and pepper
pinch of paprika
2 tbsp Parmesan cheese, grated

Preheat the oven to 190°C/375°F/Gas Mark 5.

Remove the crusts from the bread and press them into the cups of a muffin tin. Brush well with melted butter.

Beat the eggs well in a medium-sized mixing bowl. Stir in the milk. Add the onion, courgette, cheese, crumbs, basil and seasoning. Mix well.

Carefully pour the egg mixture into the bread cases. Sprinkle with the paprika and Parmesan cheese, then place the tin in the oven and bake for about 45 minutes, or until set and golden.

Turn off the oven, but leave the toasties to cool for 10 minutes before transferring to a serving platter.

nibbles

These are the small dishes, appropriate for any finger food occasion, but not meals in themselves unless made in larger quantities or, better yet, served with a host of companion nibbles. Mix and match them, make some hot and some cold, offer them with a selection of bread, crisps, raw vegetables and sauces to dip into. Let your imagination go wild and have a tasty time.

bite-sized barbecued
spare ribs

easy	
serves 4	
10 minutes	
20 minutes	

ingredients

SAUCE
50 ml/2 fl oz plum, hoisin, sweet
  & sour or duck sauce
1 tsp brown sugar
1 tbsp tomato ketchup
pinch of garlic powder
2 tbsp dark soy sauce

1 kg/2 lb 4oz spare ribs, chopped
  into 5 cm/2 inch pieces

3 tbsp fresh, torn coriander, to garnish

Preheat the oven to 190°C/375°F/Gas Mark 5.

To make the sauce, combine the plum or other sauce,
brown sugar, ketchup, garlic powder and soy sauce in a large
mixing bowl.

Add the spare ribs to the sauce and stir to coat them thoroughly.
Transfer to a metal roasting pan and arrange in a single layer.

Place the roasting pan in the oven and cook the ribs for
20 minutes, or until they are cooked through and sticky. Arrange
on a large platter and serve immediately, garnished with coriander.

devilled eggs

		ingredients
	very easy	8 hardboiled eggs
	serves 4	2 tbsp tuna fish
		4 anchovy fillets
	10 minutes	6 black olives, stoned
	—	1 tsp capers

Peel the eggs, cut in half lengthways and remove the yolks. Mash the yolks, or put in the food processor, along with the tuna, 2 anchovies, 4 olives and all of the capers.

Blend the ingredients together to make a smooth paste, adding 1 teaspoon of oil from the tuna or anchovies, or some extra-virgin olive oil, to achieve the correct consistency.

Arrange the egg whites on an attractive serving dish. Fill the gaps with the yolk mixture using either a teaspoon or a piping bag. Make sure the filling is piled high.

Garnish the filled eggs with the remaining anchovies and olives (cut into tiny strips) and serve.

fresh figs
with gorgonzola

		ingredients
	very easy	8 slices baguette, ciabatta or bloomer
	serves 4	115 g/4 oz Gorgonzola or other strong blue cheese, sliced or crumbled
	5 minutes	4 fresh figs, sliced thinly
	8–10 minutes	

Preheat the grill. Place the bread on the grill pan and toast until golden on one side. Remove the pan.

Turn the bread over and sprinkle with cheese, making sure that it covers each slice right to the edge.

Arrange the figs on top of the cheese.

Return the pan to the grill and cook for 3–4 minutes, or until the cheese is soft and the fruit is hot. Transfer to an attractive dish and serve immediately.

chorizo & olive frittata

		ingredients	
easy	55 g/2 oz butter	8 large eggs
	1 small onion, chopped finely	2 tbsp milk
serves 4	1 small green or red pepper,	salt and pepper
	deseeded and chopped finely	55 g/2 oz Cheddar cheese, grated
	2 tomatoes, deseeded and diced	
	2 small cooked potatoes, diced	GARNISH
10 minutes	125 g/4½ oz chorizo or salami,	mixed salad leaves
	chopped finely	pimento strips
	8 green or black olives, pitted	
15 minutes	and chopped finely	

Melt the butter over a medium heat in a large frying pan. Add the onion, pepper and tomatoes. Stir well to coat in butter, then cook for 3–4 minutes, or until soft. Mix in the potatoes, chorizo and olives. Cook gently for 5 minutes to heat through.

In a small bowl, beat the eggs with the milk, salt and pepper. Pour over the vegetables in the pan and reduce the heat to low. Cook the eggs, occasionally lifting the edges and tilting the pan to let the liquid run to the outside.

Preheat the grill to high. When the eggs are mostly set, with only a small wet patch in the middle, sprinkle over the cheese. Place the pan under the grill and cook for 2 minutes, or until the cheese has melted and is golden brown. Remove the pan from the grill and let the fritatta cool before cutting into wedges. Garnish with salad leaves and strips of pimento and serve.

falafel

<table>
<tr>
<td>easy</td>
<td colspan="2">**ingredients**</td>
</tr>
<tr>
<td rowspan="2">serves 4</td>
<td>
225 g/8 oz dried chickpeas
cold water, to cover
1 large onion, chopped finely
1 garlic clove, crushed
salt
cayenne pepper
2 tbsp chopped fresh parsley
2 tsp ground cumin
2 tsp ground coriander
</td>
<td>
½ tsp baking powder
oil, for deep frying

SERVING SUGGESTIONS
hummus (see page 8)
sesame aubergine dip (see page 12)
pitta bread
tomato wedges
</td>
</tr>
<tr>
<td>1 hour
+ 1 hour
to rest</td>
</tr>
<tr>
<td>25 minutes –
1 hour
10 minutes</td>
<td></td>
<td></td>
</tr>
</table>

Soak the chickpeas overnight in enough cold water to cover them and allow room for expansion. Drain the chickpeas and boil in fresh water until tender, about 1 hour (or 15 minutes, if using a pressure cooker). Drain.

To make the falafel, put the chickpeas into a food processor and blend to make a coarse paste. Add the onion, garlic, seasoning and baking powder and blend again to mix thoroughly.

Leave the mixture to rest for 30 minutes, then shape into 8 patties and arrange on a plate. Leave to rest for a further 30 minutes.

Heat the oil in a wok or deep pan. Gently drop in the patties and cook until golden brown. Carefully remove from the oil and drain for a few minutes on a plate lined with kitchen paper.

Serve hot or at room temperature with a selection of dips, accompanied by tomato wedges or sandwiched into pitta bread.

cheesy corn puffs

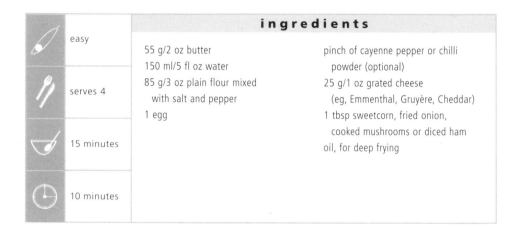

		ingredients	
easy	55 g/2 oz butter	pinch of cayenne pepper or chilli
	150 ml/5 fl oz water	powder (optional)
serves 4	85 g/3 oz plain flour mixed	25 g/1 oz grated cheese
	with salt and pepper	(eg, Emmenthal, Gruyère, Cheddar)
	1 egg	1 tbsp sweetcorn, fried onion,
15 minutes		cooked mushrooms or diced ham
		oil, for deep frying
10 minutes		

To make the choux pastry, place the butter and water in a small pan. Heat until the water boils, then remove from the heat, add the seasoned flour and mix well until it forms a ball that leaves the side of the pan clean. Beat in the egg, a little bit at a time, until it has all been absorbed.

Season the pastry with cayenne (if using) and stir in the cheese and whichever flavourings you choose.

Heat the oil in a wok or deep pan. Gently drop small spoonfuls of the pastry into the oil. Cook until golden brown and well puffed. Carefully remove from the oil and drain for a few minutes on a plate lined with kitchen paper. Serve immediately.

miniature chicken kebabs

easy	
serves 4	
15 minutes + 30 minutes to marinate	
10 minutes	

ingredients

SWEET & SOUR MARINADE
125 ml/4 fl oz orange, grapefruit or
pineapple juice
1 tbsp sweet sherry
50 ml/2 fl oz dark soy sauce
50 ml/2 fl oz chicken stock
2 tbsp cider vinegar
1 tsp tomato purée
2 tbsp light brown sugar
pinch of ground ginger

1 chicken breast, skinned, boned and
cut into 1 cm/½ inch pieces
½ small onion, cut into
1 cm/½ inch pieces
½ red pepper, cut into
1 cm/½ inch pieces
½ green pepper, cut into
1 cm/½ inch pieces

To make the marinade, combine all the liquid ingredients in a mixing bowl. Add the tomato purée, sugar and ginger. Mix well, then add the chicken and vegetables and stir to coat thoroughly.

Cover the bowl with clingfilm and place in the refrigerator to marinate for 30 minutes.

Drain off the marinade and reserve. Place alternating pieces of chicken and vegetables on cocktail sticks, taking care not to pack them too tightly together.

Preheat a griddle or heavy frying pan over a high heat. Place the kebabs in the pan and cook, turning frequently, for about 10 minutes, or until gently browned and cooked through. Baste occasionally with the reserved marinade.

Pile the kebabs high on platters and serve immediately.

miniature
beef kebabs

easy

serves 4

10 minutes
+ 30 minutes
to marinate

5 minutes

ingredients

SPICY TOMATO MARINADE
50 ml/2 fl oz tomato juice
50 ml/2 fl oz beef stock
1 tbsp Worcestershire sauce
1 tbsp lemon juice
2 tbsp dry sherry
few drops of Tabasco sauce
2 tbsp vegetable oil
1 tbsp minced celery

115 g/4 oz sirloin or rump steak, cut
  into cubes about 1 cm/½ inch in size
4 button mushrooms, cut into cubes
  about 1 cm/½ inch in size
½ small onion, cut into cubes about
  1 cm/½ inch in size

Combine all the ingredients for the marinade in a large mixing bowl, whisk well and stir in the meat, mushrooms and onion. Cover the bowl with clingfilm and place in the refrigerator to marinate for 30 minutes.

Drain off the marinade and reserve. Place alternating pieces of steak and vegetables on cocktail sticks, taking care not to pack them too tightly together.

Preheat a griddle or heavy frying pan over a high heat. Place the kebabs in the pan and cook, turning frequently, until gently browned and cooked through – 5 minutes. Baste occasionally with the reserved marinade.

Pile the kebabs high on platters and serve immediately.

mixed vegetable fritters

		ingredients	
easy	BATTER	1 large sweet onion, sliced thickly,
	175 g/6 oz plain flour	rings separated
serves 4	½ tsp baking powder	1 large courgette, cut into batons
	pinch of salt	1 small aubergine, cut into batons
	1 egg	1 small cauliflower, cut into florets
15 minutes	125 ml/4 fl oz milk	115 g/4 oz button mushrooms,
	½ tsp Tabasco sauce	stems trimmed off level with caps
	(optional)	
		lemon wedges, to garnish
15 minutes	oil, for deep frying	garlicky tomato sauce, to serve

To prepare the batter, combine the dry ingredients in a large mixing bowl. Add the egg, beating to eliminate lumps. Gradually add the milk, stirring constantly. Add Tabasco sauce (if using).

Heat the oil in a wok or deep pan. Dip the vegetables into the batter, then lift out and let any excess drip back into the bowl. Gently drop into the wok and cook until golden brown. Carefully remove from the oil and drain for a few minutes on a plate lined with kitchen paper.

Serve hot, garnished with lemon wedges or accompanied by a garlicky tomato sauce for dipping.

parsley fish balls

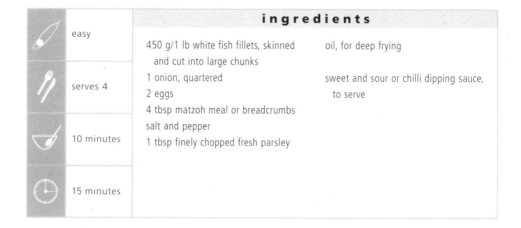

		ingredients	
easy		450 g/1 lb white fish fillets, skinned and cut into large chunks	oil, for deep frying
serves 4		1 onion, quartered 2 eggs 4 tbsp matzoh meal or breadcrumbs salt and pepper	sweet and sour or chilli dipping sauce, to serve
10 minutes		1 tbsp finely chopped fresh parsley	
15 minutes			

Place the fish and onion in a food processor. Blend to make a coarse paste, then put the paste into a large mixing bowl.

Add the eggs and matzoh meal (or breadcrumbs, if using) and stir to bind. Season with salt, pepper and parsley.

Heat the oil in a wok or deep pan.

Shape the fish into small balls or patties and gently drop into the oil. Cook until golden brown. Carefully remove from the oil and drain for a few minutes on a plate lined with kitchen paper.

Serve the fish hot or at room temperature, accompanied by sweet and sour or chilli sauce for dipping.

prawn balls

		ingredients	
	extremely easy	450 g/1 lb prawns	½ tsp salt
		6–10 water chestnuts	oil, for deep frying
		1 tbsp minced onion	
	serves 4	1 tsp finely grated fresh ginger	sweet and sour, chilli or sweet soy
		1 egg, beaten	sauce, to serve
	5 minutes + 30 minutes to chill	2 tbsp cornflour	
		1 tbsp dry sherry	lemon slices, to garnish
	10 minutes		

Put the prawns, water chestnuts, onion and ginger in a food processor and blend to make a thick paste. Transfer to a mixing bowl and add the egg, cornflour, sherry and salt. Mix well. Cover the bowl with clingfilm and chill for 30 minutes.

Meanwhile, shape the prawn paste into small balls. Heat the oil in a wok or deep pan. Drop the balls gently into the oil and cook until golden brown. Carefully remove from the oil and drain for a few minutes on a plate lined with kitchen paper.

Serve the prawn balls hot with a sweet and sour, chilli or sweet soy sauce for dipping or garnished lemon slices.

buttered herby
new potatoes

		ingredients
very easy		12 small new potatoes
serves 4		115 g/4 oz cup butter
10 minutes		2 tbsp finely minced fresh rosemary
20 minutes		salt and pepper

Boil the potatoes in salted water until just tender. Drain well.

Melt the butter in a large, heavy pan. Add the rosemary and the potatoes and mix well. Continue cooking, stirring frequently, for 5 minutes, or until the potatoes are thoroughly coated in rosemary butter and are starting to brown.

Arrange the potatoes on large platters, sprinkle with salt and pepper and serve immediately.

savoury rice balls

extremely easy	**ingredients**
serves 4	55 g/2 oz cooked rice or plain risotto / 175 g/6 oz white crabmeat, flaked / 3 spring onions, chopped finely / 2 tbsp mayonnaise / 55 g/2 oz grated cheese / (eg, mozzarella, Fontina or Gruyère)
20 minutes + at least 2½ hours to chill	pinch of cayenne pepper / 1 tbsp fresh parsley, chopped finely / 2 eggs / 25 g/1 oz plain flour / bread crumbs, to coat / oil, for deep frying
10 minutes	

Combine the rice, crabmeat, spring onions, mayonnaise, cheese, cayenne, parsley and one egg in a large bowl. Mix well. Cover the bowl with clingfilm and refrigerate for at least 2 hours, but overnight if possible.

Take spoonfuls of the mixture and roll, with wet hands, into small balls. Cover as before and chill for a further 30 minutes.

Heat the oil over a high heat in a large wok or deep pan.

Meanwhile, beat the remaining egg. Gently roll the rice balls in flour, then quickly dip them in beaten egg. Coat thoroughly and drain off any excess.

Roll the rice balls in bread crumbs. Press the crumbs in firmly but gently, shake off any loose crumbs, then fry for about 5 minutes, or until crisp and golden. Drain well and serve either hot or cold.

crunchy potato skins

		ingredients
easy		4 potatoes, cooked in their skins
		2 rashers of streaky bacon
serves 4		115 g/4 oz blue cheese, crumbled
		oil, for deep frying
10 minutes		crème fraîche or soured cream, to garnish
5 minutes		

Cut the potatoes in half and scoop out the soft inside, leaving a lining about ½ cm/¼ inch thick.

Grill the bacon until crisp. Transfer to a plate and cut into small strips. Combine the blue cheese and bacon in a small mixing bowl.

Heat the oil over a high heat in a wok or deep pan. Carefully drop the potato skins into the oil and fry for 3–4 minutes, or until crisp and golden. Remove and drain well on kitchen paper.

Arrange the potato skins on a large plate and fill each with a spoonful of the bacon and cheese mixture, piling it high so it is almost overflowing. Garnish with a teaspoon of crème fraîche or soured cream and serve immediately.

oven-fried
chicken wings

		ingredients	
very easy		12 chicken wings	1 tsp paprika
		1 egg	salt and pepper
serves 4		50 ml/2 fl oz milk	225 g/8 oz breadcrumbs
		4 heaped tbsp plain flour	55 g/2 oz butter
15 minutes			
20 minutes			

Separate the chicken wings into 3 pieces each. Discard the bony tip. Beat the egg with the milk in a shallow dish. Combine the flour, paprika, salt and pepper in a shallow dish. Place the breadcrumbs in a shallow dish.

Preheat the oven to 220°C/425°F/Gas Mark 7.

Dip the chicken pieces into the egg, coat well, then drain and dredge in flour. Remove, shaking off any excess, and roll in crumbs, pressing them in gently, then shaking off any excess.

Melt the butter in the oven in a shallow roasting tin large enough to hold all the chicken pieces in a single layer. Arrange the chicken, skin side down, in the butter and bake for 10 minutes. Turn and bake for a further 10 minutes.

Remove the chicken from the tin and arrange on a large platter. Serve hot or at room temperature.

crispy bacon nibbles

		ingredients
extremely easy		12 rashers of streaky bacon
serves 4		12 dates, prunes, scallops
10 minutes		or water chestnuts
5–30 minutes		

Holding the bacon down firmly with a knife or fork on a cutting board, use a sharp knife to smooth and stretch the length.

Place a date, scallop or water chestnut at one end of each rasher and roll up. Secure with a cocktail stick to keep it closed.

Preheat a ridged griddle or grill until very hot. Place the bacon rolls in the pan or on the grill rack and cook, turning once, for 5–10 minutes, or until the bacon is crisp and well browned. Whatever is wrapped in the bacon must be thoroughly cooked or heated through. Alternatively, you could cook the bacon rolls on a flat baking tray for 25–30 minutes in an oven preheated to 200°C/400°F/Gas Mark 6.

Transfer to a large platter and serve immediately.

ham & parmesan pinwheels

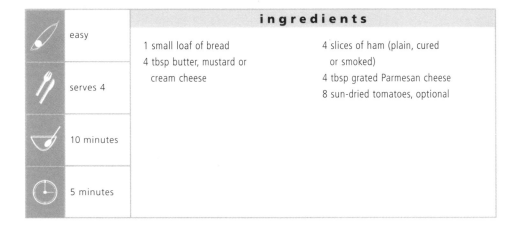

		ingredients
easy	1 small loaf of bread	4 slices of ham (plain, cured
	4 tbsp butter, mustard or	or smoked)
serves 4	cream cheese	4 tbsp grated Parmesan cheese
		8 sun-dried tomatoes, optional
10 minutes		
5 minutes		

Remove the crusts from the bread and cut into four slices lengthways. Place each slice between two pieces of greaseproof paper and flatten with a rolling pin. Remove the paper.

Preheat the oven to 180°C/350°F/Gas Mark 4.

Spread each slice of bread with butter, mustard or cream cheese and top with slices of ham. Sprinkle Parmesan cheese over the top. If you are using sun-dried tomatoes, chop them and scatter over the cheese.

Roll up the bread along its length, then cut into 1 cm/½ inch slices crossways. Place the pinwheels, cut side up, on a greased baking tray. Transfer to the oven and bake for 5 minutes, or until the cheese has melted. Remove from the oven, place on a dish and serve either hot or cold.

hot salsa nachos

		ingredients	
	extremely easy	2 packs of nachos or tortilla chips	TO SERVE
		4 tbsp jalapeño peppers, sliced finely	tomato salsa
		115 g/4 oz Cheddar cheese, grated	guacamole
	serves 4		soured cream
		2 tbsp finely chopped fresh coriander, to garnish	
	5 minutes		
	10 minutes		

Preheat the oven to 190°C/375°F/Gas Mark 5.

Tip the nachos into a shallow ovenproof dish. Sprinkle with the peppers and top with the cheese. Bake for 5–10 minutes to melt the cheese.

Remove the nachos from the oven, garnish with coriander and serve with salsa, guacamole and a dish of soured cream.

index